FAMOUS ARTISTS

MATISSE

The author, Antony Mason, is a freelance editor and author of
many books for children.

Designer	Tessa Barwick
Editor	Sarah Levete
Picture research	Brooks Krikler Research
Illustrators	Michaela Stewart
	Tessa Barwick

First edition for the United States, Canada, and the Philippines published 1995 by Barron's Educational Series, Inc.

© Aladdin Books Ltd 1995
All rights reserved

Designed and produced by
Aladdin Books Ltd
28 Percy Street
London W1P 0LD

First published in
Great Britain in 1995 by
Watts Books
96 Leonard Street
London EC2A 4RH

All inquiries should be addressed to:
Barron's Educational Series, Inc.
250 Wireless Boulevard
Hauppauge, New York 11788

International Standard Book No. 0-8120-6534-4 (hardcover) 0-8120-9426-3 (paperback)

Library of Congress Catalog Card No.: 95-22839

Library of Congress Cataloging-in-Publication Data
Mason, Antony.
Matisse / Antony Mason.
p. cm.–(Famous artists)
Includes index
Summary: Explores the French painter's life and development as an artist, his involvement with Fauvism, and his continued experimentation with art.
ISBN 0-8120-6534-4 (hardcover) – ISBN 0-8120-9426-3 (paperback)
1. Matisse, Henri, 1869-1954–Juvenile literature. 2. Artists–France–Biography–Juvenile literature. 3. Art appreciation–Juvenile literature. [1. Matisse, Henri, 1869-1954. 2. Artists. 3. Painting, French. 4. Art appreciation.] I. Title.
II. Series.

N6853.M33M36 1995
759.4–dc20
[B]
95-22839
CIP
AC
Printed in Belgium
5678 4208 987654321

FAMOUS ARTISTS

MATISSE

ANTONY MASON

BARRON'S

CONTENTS

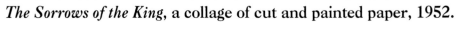

The Sorrows of the King, a collage of cut and painted paper, 1952.

INTRODUCTION

Henri Matisse (1869-1954) is considered to be one of the greatest and most inventive artists of the twentieth century. For a time, he was at the forefront of a group of artists known as the "Fauves" whose paintings were renowned for their bold and unusual use of color. Matisse worked hard to achieve the sense of movement and simplicity of design for which his paintings, sculptures, and book illustrations became famous. Even in old age, Matisse created some of his most imaginative works, using sheets of cut paper. This book explores Matisse's development, from his discovery of painting and his training in Paris to his final years in the south of France. His techniques are also discussed, and you can try some of them for yourself. Below you can see how the book is organized.

Illustration of the artist's home or environment

The story of the artist's life

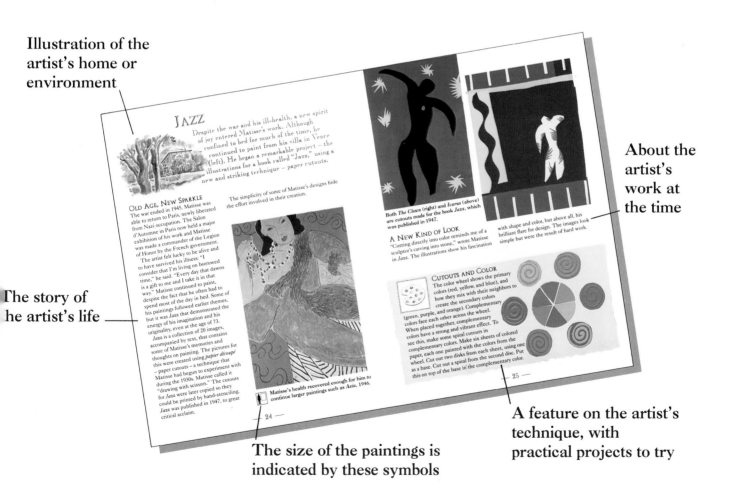

About the artist's work at the time

A feature on the artist's technique, with practical projects to try

The size of the paintings is indicated by these symbols

DISCOVERING ART

As a young man, Matisse trained to be a lawyer. It was only at the age of 20, when he was recovering from appendicitis, that he realized that the pastime of painting was to become his passion in life. In 1891, Matisse abandoned his career in law, and went to study painting and drawing in Paris (left), the art capital of the world.

AN ORDINARY CHILDHOOD

Henri Matisse was born on December 31, 1869, at his grandfather's house in Le Cateau-Cambrésis, a small town in northern France. His father was a grain merchant and his mother was a hatmaker. At the age of 17, Matisse studied law in Paris, returning to his hometown, Bohain, to work as a lawyer's clerk. He found the work dull, and to relieve the boredom he took art classes. In 1890, when he was confined to bed by illness, his mother gave him a set of paints. For the first time, Matisse took painting seriously.

 Still Life after de Heem's Dessert, 1893, a skillful copy of a work by a seventeenth-century artist.

Here Matisse shows his interest in filling his composition with strong shapes. At the start of his career, he copied the techniques of early French and Dutch painters. Later, he filled his paintings with brighter colors, and he used dark colors for outlines only.

 Woman Reading, 1894, was one of the first of Matisse's works to be exhibited.

LEARNING THE TRADE

"Once bitten by the demon of painting," he later wrote, "I never wanted to give up."

In 1891, against his father's wishes, Matisse headed for Paris to begin his artistic training. Failing to secure a place at the prestigious École des Beaux-Arts, he went instead to the Académie Julian. Here he met the painter Albert Marquet, who became a lifelong friend. The Académie was run by a respected artist named Adolphe-William Bouguereau. Although Matisse appreciated learning the traditional skills of drawing from Bouguereau, he felt restricted by his old-fashioned approach.

At the age of 23, Matisse decided to join the more lively studio run by Gustave Moreau, a well-known painter. Moreau encouraged Matisse to copy the work of the Old Masters in the great museums of Paris.

STILL LIFE

A still life is a painting of everyday objects. Choose your subject – a bowl of fruit, perhaps – and decide how you want to arrange it. Do you want to include any background material to add to the image – perhaps a brightly colored tablecloth? Study the composition, looking carefully at the texture, shape, and color of your objects. You could experiment with different styles. One version could be a detailed and realistic portrayal of the objects; another could be more abstract, conveying their shapes and colors.

A Style of His Own

At the age of 25, Matisse was at last accepted by the École des Beaux-Arts. Soon after, he got married and had three young children to support. To make ends meet, he worked as a decorator and his wife, Amélie, worked as a milliner, making hats. Matisse's own paintings were influenced by the Impressionists, particularly in the way that he used light in his work.

A Young Family

Matisse (above) was a serious young man with a neatly trimmed beard and glasses. In 1898 he married Amélie Parayre, who adopted his four-year-old daughter, Marguerite, born to his former girlfriend Caroline Joblaud. Matisse and Amélie honeymooned in London, returning to France via Corsica. By 1900 they had two sons, Jean and Pierre. After Gustave Moreau's death in 1898, Matisse set up his own studio. But still eager to learn, he took a course in sculpture.

In *Dinner Table*, 1897, Matisse focuses on the effect of light.

The influence of other artists' styles on Matisse is evident here. He uses dabs of pure, bright color in the background, which recall the Impressionists' painting of light. The tiny dots of color are similar to the technique used by the Pointillists.

Orange Still Life, 1899, shows Matisse's fascination with light.

DEVELOPING HIS OWN STYLE

Matisse studied the work of other modern artists, exploring their techniques and styles to see how they suited his own ideas. He greatly admired the Post-Impressionist Paul Cézanne, who broke landscapes up into slabs of color. Matisse even sold his wedding ring to buy Cézanne's painting, the *Three Bathers*.

Matisse found inspiration from his travels. The light of the Mediterranean was to be a continuing influence on his work. In 1904 an important art dealer, Ambroise Vollard, held an exhibition of Matisse's paintings in Paris.

PAINTING THE LIGHT

Experiment with capturing light like the Impressionists. Work quickly, using little dashes, short brushstrokes or tiny dots of bright color to give the impression of sparkling light, or of light dancing on water. For light areas, use bright colors – yellow, orange, and white. For darker areas, put dots of darker color – such as deep orange and red – next to each other. Try adding touches of a surprising color, such as green. But you don't need to mix the colors. Your eyes will do the mixing for you!

THE WILD ONES

By 1901 Matisse had met two young artists, André Derain and Maurice Vlaminck. He was attracted by their lively ideas about art; Vlaminck had even declared that he wanted "to burn down the Louvre." Together, the three artists headed a radical new style that became known as Fauvism.

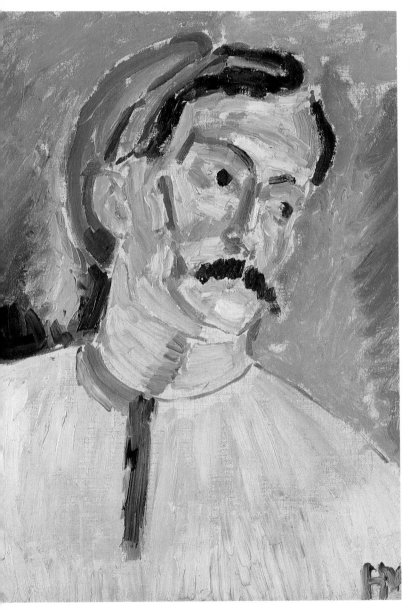

Matisse's *Portrait of André Derain*, 1905, shows the vigorous, rapid painting style for which the Fauves became famous.

A CHANGE OF MOOD

For awhile, Matisse and Amélie were in low spirits, struggling with money worries and health problems. In 1903, in order to help resolve their financial difficulties, the family left Paris to stay with Matisse's parents in Bohain.

But the summer of 1905 saw a change in the artist's mood. He and his family were staying in a Mediterranean fishing village named Collioure (above), near the Spanish border. Here they were joined by André Derain and Maurice Vlaminck.

When the three artists returned to Paris to take part in a major annual exhibition of new art, the Salon d'Automne, their work caused a sensation. Nothing like this had been seen before. The paintings were colorful, vigorous, and bold. The critic Louis Vauxcelles thought it looked like the work of wild beasts (*fauves*). The painters rather enjoyed this description and adopted the name. From 1905 to 1908 Fauvism dominated the modern art scene in Europe, before being overshadowed by a new movement, Cubism.

Throughout his life, Matisse never felt tied down to one particular style; he was always open to new ideas. In 1906, when he made his first trip to North Africa, the artist was already beginning to look for sources of inspiration that would lead him away from the wildness of the Fauves.

A BLAZE OF COLOR

Fauvism was a movement of a loosely knit group of like-minded artists who rejected the subtle and delicate style of the Impressionists. The Fauves made little attempt to represent landscapes and people as they really appeared. Instead, they played around with the way that we see the world. They used bright, bold colors and shapes, applied in rapid, vigorous brushstrokes. Perspective was not important, and their images often looked like flat surfaces.

 *The Open Window*, painted in 1905, shows how the Fauves used bold and surprising colors, applied to the canvas in strong brushstrokes.

Matisse was more concerned with the color and design of the landscape than in copying exactly how it looked. In the style of the Fauves, he freely applies paint, creating unusual and striking combinations of primary and secondary colors. (See page 25).

INSTANT FAUVISM

Become a Fauve! Fold a piece of paper in half so that you have a dividing line down the middle. Choose a simple subject such as a tree; draw it in the center of the page so that the middle of the page divides your subject in two. Paint one side of it with realistic colors. Paint the other side in the Fauvist style, with crude, thick outlines in unexpected colors. Experiment with different combinations of color. What is the effect of using complementary colors (see page 25) next to each other?

NEW DIRECTIONS

Matisse's travels through Europe, Africa, and the islands of the South Pacific awakened his interest in different styles and forms. Although he had left behind the "wildness" of Fauvism, Matisse's innovative work continued to cause controversy. Despite this, at the age of 39 Matisse was recognized as an outstanding artist.

TEACHER AND LEADER

Now a successful artist whose work was exhibited in Berlin, New York, Stockholm, Moscow, and London, Matisse set up his own private painting academy in Paris in 1908. This was attended by young artists from all over Europe. But three years later, Matisse decided to close the school so that he could concentrate on his own paintings. In 1909 Matisse's family moved from Paris to a larger house and studio in a suburb of Paris, Issy-les-Moulineaux. He traveled frequently to Germany and Spain (above left), to study work by the Islamic artists of the past, which he admired for its subtle patterns and colors. He filled the family home with the textiles and ceramics he had collected on his travels.

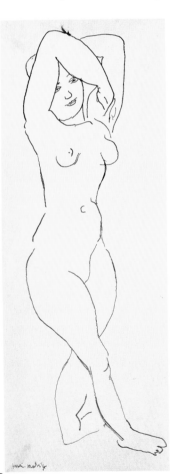

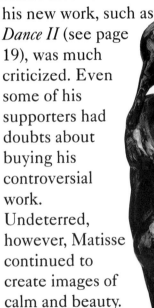
Standing Nude, pen and ink drawing, 1907–08.

Matisse was fascinated by sculpture from other cultures, such as Africa and the South Pacific, admiring its strong, expressive shapes. During his lifetime, he made about 70 sculptures. He also began to look at ways of presenting scenes as flat images, filled with the colors and patterns of a scene but without the dramatic strokes of Fauvism.

But it was a difficult time for Matisse. His father died in 1910 and some of his new work, such as *Dance II* (see page 19), was much criticized. Even some of his supporters had doubts about buying his controversial work. Undeterred, however, Matisse continued to create images of calm and beauty.

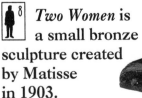
Two Women is a small bronze sculpture created by Matisse in 1903.

Color is more important here than the representation of a realistic image. Compare this to Matisse's treatment of a similar theme in *Dinner Table,* on page 8. Here the wall and table are covered in the same pattern.

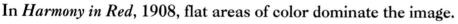

In *Harmony in Red*, 1908, flat areas of color dominate the image.

PAINTING FLAT

Early Renaissance artists, who Matisse had studied on his travels to Italy in 1907 and 1908, did not know the rules of perspective. Matisse did, but he deliberately chose to ignore them. He was more interested in filling his paintings with color rather than in creating scenes with depth. Matisse often constructed images and patterns out of pure color. Such flat areas of paint, applied without using perspective, were later to become a feature of Matisse's innovative technique of paper cutouts.

OUT OF PERSPECTIVE

Objects look smaller the further away they are. Perspective gives this sense of depth to an artist's work. Lines which in real life run

parallel appear to meet at a single point in the distance – the "vanishing point" (above).

Experiment with painting the same scene using perspective and then painting flat, without perspective (left). Notice the new and interesting shapes you can create.

NORTH AFRICA

With his school closed, Matisse was able to devote more time to his art and travels. In 1912, he began the first of two long trips to Morocco (left), which had a profound influence on his painting. Matisse's work became colored with a new sense of light and calm. But back in France a new movement – Cubism – was taking the art world by storm.

MOROCCAN LIGHTS

In 1908 Matisse had written that "a work of art must be harmonious in its entirety." By contrast, the work of the Cubists, led by the young and energetic Pablo Picasso, was dark and angular; images were broken up into geometrical shapes. Although they held different views about painting, Matisse and Picasso became good friends, visiting each other's studios and exchanging paintings.

From 1912 to 1913 Matisse spent much time in Morocco. He reflected the images and colors of the Moroccan landscape in his paintings. The artist was also entranced by the beauty of the south of France, where he stayed for a while with his mother, who was suffering from heart trouble. But in 1913 Matisse decided to return to Paris.

In July 1914 a large retrospective exhibition of his work was held in Berlin, but Europe was on the brink of conflict. In August, war was declared; Germany invaded Belgium and France. World War I had begun.

Matisse, now 44 years old, applied to do military service but was not accepted. His health was still troublesome. He traveled back to Collioure, where he and his family remained until November 1914. There he met the Cubist artist Juan Gris and even adopted some of Gris's ideas.

In 1917 Matisse's sons, Jean and Pierre, left to join the army. The family was growing apart. Matisse now put more energy into his work.

Window at Tangier, painted in 1912.

SHADES OF BLUE AND PINK

The paintings from this period show Matisse exploring shape and color to create a mood of calm. His paintings of North Africa are very sparse, with simple compositions and limited color schemes. But he creates a sense of space and tranquillity through simple, flat areas of color, often shades of blue and pink.

The blue light of Morocco is reflected in the triptych (a set of three pictures) *Zorah on the Terrace*, 1912 (left), *Entrance to the Kasbah*, 1912 (below), and *Window at Tangier*, 1912 (bottom left).

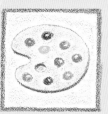

FRAMES WITHIN FRAMES

Capturing images through a frame, such as a window or door, helps to draw the eye through to the view. Try to paint a view through a window frame. Pencil in the outline of the window, and sketch in the details of the view. Paint the distant parts of the view with light colors. Use darker colors for objects that are nearest to you. The "vanishing point" (see page 13) will help to add depth to your scene.

ODALISQUES

In 1917, Matisse moved to Nice
(right), a seaside town in southeastern
France. For many years after this he lived
between Paris and the south of France.
Matisse began a series of paintings of
"odalisques," which recall the exotic world of
the East.

THE WARMTH OF THE SOUTH

As the war drew to a close in 1918, Matisse
was living in Nice. Here he met other great
artists, such as the Impressionist Auguste
Renoir, who had also chosen to live in the
South for its light, color, and warmth.

In 1919 Matisse went to London to create
the sets and costumes for a new ballet,
performed by the Ballets Russes, one of the
most exciting troupes of the day. This
project stimulated his interest in textile
design and, later, in paper cutouts.

But the success of this work was also full of
sorrow for Matisse. The day before the
première, his mother died. Although he was
now world famous, Matisse became solitary
and depressed.

Odalisque with Red Trousers, 1921, reflects the mood of the post-war period.

Odalisque *"The White Slave,"* 1921–22.

SHAPELY FORMS AND TEXTILES

Literally, odalisques are female slaves from the Turkish harems, the luxuriously decorated rooms where the wives and mistresses of rich men lived.

But Matisse was more interested in creating a mood rather than in showing highly realistic images of women. His odalisques evoke an oriental atmosphere of calm and sleepy beauty. The women recline, half dressed, on soft couches, surrounded by beautiful textiles. Matisse creates a richness by focusing on the colors and patterns on the materials. The backgrounds are as important as the figures, but here Matisse has returned to a more traditional style of painting. The figures are shaded and rounded, and there is more use of perspective.

Odalisque in Red Trousers, 1924–25.

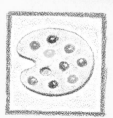

A WORLD OF PATTERNS

Curtains, carpets, and wallpaper can provide exciting and atmospheric backgrounds to your paintings. Try not to copy them too closely – the effect is created by the color and pattern, not by the detail. What about painting a figure completely surrounded in patterns – perhaps sitting on a couch next to some cushions, with a carpet below and wallpaper and curtains behind? Notice how folds in material change the patterns.

DANCE

In 1930 Alfred Barnes, an American art collector, commissioned Matisse to paint a mural for his private foundation in Merion, Pennsylvania. For this, Matisse returned to the theme of dance that had featured in his paintings twenty years earlier. The project was huge; it took three years to complete.

SUCCESS AND SORROW

In 1930 Matisse set off on an adventure, traveling to New York (above), San Francisco, and then to the island of Tahiti. In New York he met Alfred Barnes to discuss the details of the mural (a painting on a wall, or hung on a wall). The mural was to be installed beneath a row of arches at Barnes' gallery. The total length of the three-piece work, painted in oil on canvas, was over 39 feet (12 meters.) It was such a huge project that Matisse had to hire an old film studio in Nice to begin work on it.

Matisse started out with a design that was similar to *Dance II*, which he had painted in 1910. Gradually, however, the figures became bolder and more stylized. As he designed the mural, Matisse worked with huge pieces of paper and painted cutouts. He wanted to create images that would not overshadow the other works displayed in the gallery, painted by such great artists as Cézanne and Renoir.

The commission caused considerable problems. Matisse had to abandon his original mural because the measurements that he had been sent were too small! He had to begin all over again. There was a price to pay for the eventual success of the mural. The three years of labor that the artist had devoted to them weakened his health. Matisse's relationship with his wife became increasingly strained. They now led separate lives. Matisse concentrated fully on his work – paintings, sculptures, and drawings.

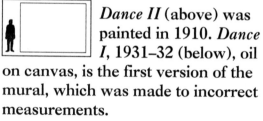

Dance II (above) was painted in 1910. *Dance I*, 1931–32 (below), oil on canvas, is the first version of the mural, which was made to incorrect measurements.

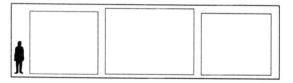

FIGURES IN MOTION

Make your paper move! Place three sheets of different-colored paper on top of each other. On the top sheet draw a large, simple figure. Hold the sheets together and cut out the figure. Separate the limbs from each of the figures and arrange them on paper. You can make each one move like a puppet – try combining different colors.

CHANGING TIMES

Europe was in growing turmoil as the aggression of the Nazis in Germany pushed the world toward war. But despite this, his poor health, and his recent separation from Amélie, Matisse continued to express calmness and tranquillity in his art. During the 1930s he also began to work on designs for tapestries (left) and to illustrate books.

ENDINGS AND BEGINNINGS

In 1937 Matisse became seriously ill and spent some time in the hospital. After this he remained in the south of France, moving to the Hotel Regina in Cimiez, high up in the hills of Nice.

Matisse now regularly painted the same model, a young and beautiful Russian woman named Lydia Delectorskaya, who had originally joined him as his secretary in 1933.

Matisse was taking a growing interest in French literature, illustrating the works of several of the great French poets. For these he produced lithographs – prints made by applying wax to stone.

Pink Nude, 1935, shows Matisse in a bolder mood than seen in the "odalisques."

FINDING THE FORM

Matisse's portrayal of women was no longer of "odalisques," clothed in rich materials. Instead, he focused on simple and directly posed figures, often nudes. He was interested in conveying the form of the body. To create *Pink Nude* (below left), Matisse made many drawings using paper cutouts. This helped him to achieve the final form, with its exaggerated limbs seeming to extend beyond the canvas, as in the *Dance* murals. The design of his work remained striking, with blocks of pure color.

The black highlights the simple but bold use of color and shape in *Reader against a Black Background*, painted in 1939.

Everything in this painting appears flat. The face is treated like a shape. Like a cartoon sketch, it is made up of simple lines, but the simplicity conveys great depth of expression.

OUTLINE

Strong outline can have a dramatic effect. To see this for yourself, try doing two paintings of a similar subject. Draw the outlines for both in pencil. In the first painting, take the color up to the pencil outlines. Use gentle shading to show any shape or shadow and the rounded forms of the objects. Fill the whole picture with color. In the second version, paint in the main outlines in thick brushstrokes, using dark colors such as black, brown, or deep mauve. Work quickly, so the outlines are bold and smooth. When the outlines are dry, fill them with color. Which do you prefer?

WORLD WAR II

In September 1939 war was declared. Matisse decided to spend the war years in southern France. At the age of 71 he had a major operation for cancer. The artist came close to death but made a remarkable recovery. In 1943, after an air raid on the Hotel Regina in Cimiez, Matisse (left) moved to Vence, a small town in the nearby hills.

THE WAR YEARS

Matisse could have left France at the start of the war, but he chose to remain in Nice. This became a part of Vichy, France, an area ruled by French politicians who had made a treaty with the German Nazis. In 1944 Amélie and Marguerite, Matisse's ex-wife and daughter, were arrested (and later released) by the Gestapo, the Nazi police, for their activities in the resistance – the movement against the German occupation in France.

The Conversation, 1941, shows a recurrent theme in Matisse's work – two people talking.

SIMPLICITY AND CALM

During the war, artists' materials were in short supply, but Matisse continued his busy life of painting and drawing. His work shows little of the strain of war. He remained true to his desire to paint pictures of calm and tranquillity: In 1908 he had written, "What I dream of is an art of balance, or purity and serenity, free of any troubling subject matter."

In this period, the women Matisse painted were often clothed in blouses and evening gowns, wearing strings of pearls, seated in their living rooms, set against rich backgrounds. But in *The Rumanian Blouse*, Matisse reverses this style. Here it is not the background pattern that dominates but the embroidery on the blouse itself. Matisse used the pattern on the blouse in several other paintings.

The Rumanian Blouse is a portrait of Lydia, painted in 1940.

There is always an element of surprise in Matisse's compositions. The background to *The Conversation* is split into two large areas of color, which adds to the sense of a two-sided conversation. The background does not quite touch the outline of the face, creating a softening effect.

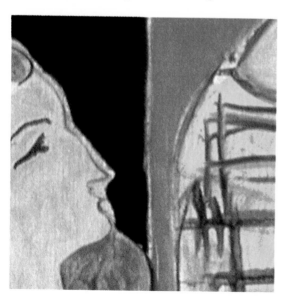

SELF-PORTRAITS

In portraits, Matisse used bold outlines, and simple lines to show facial features. To draw a picture of yourself, try sitting in front of a mirror. Work quickly to create a sense of yourself, rather than concentrating on the detail. What is the effect if you work without looking at your piece of paper?

JAZZ

Despite the war and his ill-health, a new spirit of joy entered Matisse's work. Although confined to bed for much of the time, he continued to paint from his villa in Vence (left). He began a remarkable project – the illustrations for a book called "Jazz," using a new and striking technique – paper cutouts.

OLD AGE, NEW SPARKLE

The war ended in 1945. Matisse was able to return to Paris, newly liberated from Nazi occupation. The Salon d'Automne in Paris now held a major exhibition of his work and Matisse was made a commander of the Legion of Honor by the French government.

The artist felt lucky to be alive and to have survived his illness: "I consider that I'm living on borrowed time," he said. "Every day that dawns is a gift to me and I take it in that way." Matisse continued to paint, despite the fact that he often had to spend most of the day in bed. Some of his paintings followed earlier themes, but it was *Jazz* that demonstrated the energy of his imagination and his originality, even at the age of 73.

Jazz is a collection of 20 images, accompanied by text, that contains some of Matisse's memories and thoughts on painting. The pictures for this were created using *papier découpé* – paper cutouts – a technique that Matisse had begun to experiment with during the 1930s. Matisse called it "drawing with scissors." The cutouts for *Jazz* were later copied so they could be printed by hand-stenciling. *Jazz* was published in 1947, to great critical acclaim.

The simplicity of some of Matisse's designs hide the effort involved in their creation.

Matisse's health recovered enough for him to continue larger paintings such as *Asia*, 1946.

Both *The Clown* (right) and *Icarus* (above) are cutouts made for the book *Jazz*, which was published in 1947.

A NEW KIND OF LOOK

"Cutting directly into color reminds me of a sculptor's carving into stone," wrote Matisse in *Jazz*. The illustrations show his fascination with shape and color, but above all, his brilliant flare for design. The images look simple but were the result of hard work.

CUTOUTS AND COLOR

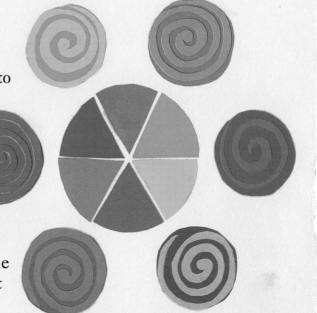

The color wheel shows the primary colors (red, yellow, and blue), and how they mix with their neighbors to create the secondary colors (green, purple, and orange). Complementary colors face each other across the wheel. When placed together, complementary colors have a strong and vibrant effect. To see this, make some spiral cutouts in complementary colors. Make six sheets of colored paper, each one painted with the colors from the wheel. Cut out two disks from each sheet, using one as a base. Cut out a spiral from the second disc. Put this on top of the base in the complementary color.

THE VENCE CHAPEL

Matisse had been nursed through his illness by a Dominican nun named Sister Jacques. In 1948 she asked if he would be interested in designing some stained-glass windows for a new chapel in Vence. Matisse gladly accepted the challenge. Although he was bedridden for much of the time (left), he continued to create masterpieces.

A NEW LEASE ON LIFE

Now nearly 80, Matisse was determined to continue working. He found that he could design and paint from his bed by using a brush attached to a bamboo pole.

The end of World War II saw many artists turn their attention to religious themes, as if they wanted to find some meaning in life after the devastation and destruction of the war years. Although he was not a follower of any particular faith, Matisse had always felt that his art was in some way an expression of a religious feeling. In 1948 Matisse contributed paintings to a new church called Notre-Dame-de-Toute-Grâce at Assy. That same year, at the request of Sister Jacques, he began work on the chapel at Vence.

But Matisse did not simply work on the stained glass – he took over the entire decoration of the chapel, designing the murals and even the priest's robes and the crucifix. He felt that "this is essentially a work of art...The essential thing is to put oneself in a frame of mind which is close to that of prayer." Matisse was delighted with the result of his work on the chapel, saying, "I consider it my masterpiece."

Large Red Interior, painted in 1948.

— 26 —

Matisse kept the designs very simple – black lines against white. Later these images were transferred in black enamel paint onto white ceramic tiles. Light is reflected from the cutout patterns of the stained glass.

The altar and mural at the Chapel of the Rosary in Vence.

PAINTING WITH LIGHT

The essential color of the interior of the Matisse chapel is white; during the daytime the floor and walls become dappled with the soft colored light cast by the stained glass.

Simplicity and spontaneity were always strong features of Matisse's paintings. In 1948 he wrote: "I have always...wished my works to have the lightness and joyousness of springtime, which never lets anyone suspect the labors it has cost."

MURALS

Try designing one – but you don't need to paint the wall! Like Matisse, you can design a mural on paper.

Use the largest sheet of paper that you can find – perhaps the back of a leftover roll of wallpaper. Pin this to the wall. Create a large, bold pattern with a strong and simple design. Try tying your paintbrush to a long stick. It may be hard to control at first, and you may need to practice, but it will help you to work on a large scale.

SPIRIT IN OLD AGE

Although Matisse's failing health prevented him from doing much painting, he continued to work energetically. In his old age, Matisse produced some of the best and most inventive work of his life. He concentrated on large-scale paper cutouts, which provided him with a new and exciting form of expression.

GENIUS TO THE LAST

In 1949 Matisse moved back to the Hotel Regina in Cimiez, where he was to spend most of the rest of his life. Soon the walls of his studio were covered with cutouts. Matisse suffered increasingly from asthma and heart trouble. Cutouts provided a way for him to continue working when his health prevented him from standing at an easel and painting. But the cutouts did not simply replace painting; they were themselves a new and important art form. He would do the cutouts himself, then from his wheelchair (above) he would direct Lydia to position the pieces on backgrounds pinned to the wall.

In 1950 he was awarded the Grand Prix at the Venice Biennale, one of the largest festivals of modern art in the world. It was a great tribute to an artist who was now 81 years old, but in fact Matisse's new work showed the youthful vigor of a man a quarter of his age.

Matisse was a kindly old man, humble about his achievements. He remained open to fresh ideas and followed developments in modern art. When he saw the new and very free abstract work by younger artists, he said that he did not understand it and so would not judge it!

In 1952 he helped to found the Musée Matisse in his birthplace, Le Cateau-Cambrésis. Matisse's last work dates from 1953, when he was 84. He died at Cimiez the following year, on November 3, 1954.

The Snail, a paper cutout created in 1953, is one of Matisse's last works.

Blue Nude IV, 1952, is in a series of blue cutouts of nudes and dancers.

COLOR AND SHAPE

Some of Matisse's last cutouts are acknowledged as his greatest masterpieces. They show his experience in composition, and his combination of colors. Some of these works are abstract; they consist of shapes, rather than recognizable images of the real world. Nonetheless, Matisse gave them names, such as *The Snail*, which tie them to things seen in the real world.

The foot of the *Blue Nude* is simplified to just three toes. Every part of the image is essential; nothing could be added or taken away without spoiling the effect.

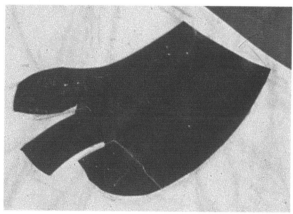

PAPER CUTOUTS

Paper cutouts make bold, strong images. They are composed of flat areas of color, so the designs have to be simple to be effective. This cutout picture (right) is made up mainly of circles and petal shapes. Try making a cutout – use printed colored paper, or select your own color range by painting sheets of paper with the colors that you want to use – make sure the paint is dry before you start cutting the shapes! Put a few sheets on top of each other to cut out lots of shapes. Experiment with realistic scenes and then abstract shapes.

CHRONOLOGY OF MATISSE'S LIFE

1869 Born on December 31 in France.

1888 Began work as a lawyer's clerk.

1891 Began art training in Paris.

1894 Marguerite born to Caroline Joblaud.

1895 Accepted by the École des Beaux-Arts, Paris.

1898 Married Amélie Parayre, who happily adopted Marguerite.

1899 Birth of their first son, Jean.

1900 Birth of their second son, Pierre.

1901 Matisse met André Derain and Maurice Vlaminck.

1904 Exhibition at Ambroise Vollard Gallery in Paris.

1905 Fauvism was given its name.

1906 First visit to North Africa. Met Picasso.

1908 The end of Fauvism.

1912-13 Two important trips to Morocco.

1925 Awarded Légion d'Honneur.

1927 Matisse awarded First Prize at the Carnegie International Exhibition in Nice.

1930-33 Painted *Dance* murals.

1939 Settled in Nice during World War II.

1941 Matisse came close to death. He never fully recovered.

1947 Publication of *Jazz*.

1950 Awarded the Grand Prix at the Venice Biennale.

1951 Completion of the chapel in Vence.

1954 Died on November 3, at Cimiez, Nice, from a heart attack.

A BRIEF HISTORY OF ART

The world's earliest works of art are figurines dating from 30,000 B.C. Cave art developed from 16,000 B.C. In the Classical Age (500-400 B.C.) sculpture flourished in Ancient Greece.

The Renaissance period began in Italy in the 1300s and reached its height in the sixteenth century. Famous Italian artists include Giotto (ca.1266-1337), Leonardo da Vinci (1452-1519), Michelangelo Buonarroti (1475-1564) and Titian (ca.1487-1576).

In Europe during the fifteenth and sixteenth centuries Hieronymus Bosch (active 1480-1516), Albrecht Dürer (1471-1528), Pieter Breughel the Elder (1525-69) and El Greco (1541-1614) produced great art. Artists of the Baroque period include Peter Paul Rubens (1577-1640) and Rembrandt van Rijn (1606-69).

During the Romantic movement, English artists J.M.W. Turner (1775-1851) and John Constable (1776-1837) produced wonderful landscapes. Francisco Goya (1746-1828) was a great Spanish portrait artist.

Impressionism began in France in the 1870s. Artists include Claude Monet (1840-1926), Camille Pissarro (1830-1903) and Edgar Degas (1834-1917). Post-Impressionists include Paul Cézanne (1839-1906), Paul Gauguin (1848-1903) and Vincent van Gogh (1853-90).

The twentieth century has seen many movements in art. Georges Braque (1882-1963) painted in the Cubist tradition, Salvador Dali (1904-89) in the Surrealist. Pablo Picasso (1881-1973) was a prolific Spanish painter. More recently Jackson Pollock (1912-56) and David Hockney (1937-) have achieved fame.

MUSEUMS AND GALLERIES

The museums and galleries listed below have examples of Matisse's work:

Musée Matisse, Nice, France

Musée Matisse, Le Cateau-Cambrésis, France

Musée National d'Art Moderne, Centre Georges Pompidou, Paris, France

Musée d'Art Moderne de la Ville de Paris, France

Musée de Peinture et de Sculpture, Grenoble, France

Tate Gallery, London, England

Museum of Modern Art, New York

Museum of Fine Arts, Boston, Massachusetts

Art Institute of Chicago, Illinois

Baltimore Museum of Art, Maryland

Barnes Foundation, Merion, Pennsylvania

Philadelphia Museum of Art, Pennsylvania

National Gallery of Canada, Ottawa

Neue Pinakothek, Munich, Germany

Staatsgalerie, Stuttgart, Germany

Statens Museum for Kunst, Copenhagen, Denmark

Pushkin Museum, Moscow, Russia

Hermitage Museum, St. Petersburg, Russia

GLOSSARY

Abstract art Paintings that consist entirely of patterns and shapes, and do not attempt to portray anything in the real world.

Complementary colors A system that divides contrasting colors into opposites, as shown by the color wheel. Each primary color has an opposing secondary color.

Cubism An art movement, dating from 1907, in which paintings and sculptures are broken up into geometric forms and shapes.

Fauve This name, relating to the French word for a wild animal, was given to a loose-knit group of artists who painted in vivid colors in about 1905-08. Matisse was considered to be the leader of the Fauves.

Flat In painting, flat refers to an area covered by a single, plain color, without shading or varying tones that might give the illusion of depth.

Impressionism The name given in the 1870s to a group of artists (Monet, Renoir, Sisley, Pissarro, and others) who evoked the passing mood of a landscape or scene by working rapidly, using quick brushstrokes.

Perspective Since the fifteenth century, artists have used perspective to suggest distance in their paintings. As a rule, objects look smaller the further away they are.

Post-Impressionism The name given to artists of the late nineteenth century whose work followed that of the Impressionists. They include Cézanne and Gauguin.

Pointillism A painting technique in which thousands of tiny dots of pure color are used to create an image. The key Pointillists were Georges Seurat and Paul Signac.

INDEX

INDEX OF PICTURES

PICTURE CREDITS:
Special thanks to Musée Matisse; Sucession Henri Matisse; Musée National d'Art Moderne, Centre Georges Pompidou; The Bridgeman Art Library; Giraudon/ Bridgeman; The Tate Gallery Publications; Frank Spooner Pictures; Design and Artists Copyrights Society; The Estate of Henri Matisse.

FIREFIGHTER CANDIDATE EXAMS

7TH EDITION

JAMES J. MURTAGH

Deputy Chief
New York City Fire Department (ret.)

and

DARRYL J. HAEFNER

Lieutenant
Bolingbrook Fire Department (ret.)
Fire Science Coordinator
College of DuPage (ret.)
Glen Ellyn, IL

BARRON'S

Acknowledgments

Thanks are due to the following for permission to reprint materials:

Cathy Briner, Employment Manager of the City of Eugene, Oregon, for *Assessment Centers for the Selection of Entry-Level Firefighters.* 1981

City of Los Angeles Police Officer and Firefighter Selection Unit for "Doing Your Best on the Firefighter Interview." Revised 1977

Palo Alto Fire Department for information about its Assessment Lab.

Donald J. Schroeder and Frank A. Lombardo for excerpts from *Police Officer Examination,* 7th ed. Copyright © 2005 by Barron's Educational Series, Inc.

Joseph P. Spinnato, Fire Commissioner, City of New York, for use of materials published in Uniformed Training and Operations *Manuals* and in Fire Prevention *Directives.*

John Wiley & Sons, Inc. for definitions from *Fire Sciences Dictionary* by Boris Kuvshinoff. Copyright © 1977 by Boris Kuvshinoff. Reprinted by permission of John Wiley & Son's, Inc.

IAFF for the information on the Candidate Physical Abilities Test (CPAT). Copyright © 1999.

We would also like to thank the following for permitting us to use test questions:

> City of Los Angeles Police Officer and Firefighter Selection Unit
> Louisville Civil Service Board
> City of Madison (WI) Fire Department
> City of New York Department of Personnel

Acknowledgment is also made to the U.S. Government Printing Office, for the use of materials from government publications.

I would like to thank James J. Murtagh for his original manuscript. I would also like to thank Capt. Mica Calfee of the Irving, TX, Fire Department for letting us use some of his definitions and the many fire departments for their invaluable information. Many fire service representatives have shared valuable resources and information. I would like to offer many thanks.

Thank you to my wife, Nancy, for putting up with me for five months, day and night, being at the computer and coming out only when *Dancing with the Stars* was on.

Darryl J. Haefner

Photo Credits: *www.shutterstock.com*: Caton Photo, pages 1, 51; Anita Patterson Peppers, page 15; Odua Images, page 61; Yuri Arcurs, page 115; Rich Koele, page 241; and Monkey Business Images, page 425.

All inquiries should be addressed to:
Barron's Educational Series, Inc.
250 Wireless Boulevard
Hauppauge, New York 11788
www.barronseduc.com

ISSN: 2167-4957
ISBN: 978-1-4380-0131-9

PRINTED IN THE UNITED STATES OF AMERICA
9 8 7 6 5 4 3 2 1

10%
POST-CONSUMER
WASTE
Paper contains a minimum
of 10% post-consumer
waste (PCW). Paper used
in this book was derived
from certified, sustainable
forestlands.